ly Peculiar
& Cheesy™

History

Jokes

& Facts

Published in Great Britain in MMXVII by
Book House, an imprint of
The Salariya Book Company Ltd
25 Marlborough Place, Brighton BN1 1UB
www.salariya.com

ISBN: 978-1-912006-52-6

SALARIYA

1 3 5 7 9 8 6 4 2

A CIP catalogue record for this book is available
from the British Library.

Printed and bound in China.
Printed on paper from sustainable sources.

Created and designed by
David Salariya.

Author:
John Townsend worked as a
secondary school teacher before
becoming a full-time writer.
He specialises in illuminating and
humorous information books for
all ages.

Artist:
David Antram studied at
Eastbourne College of Art and then
worked in advertising for 15 years
before becoming a full-time artist.
He has illustrated many children's
non-fiction books.

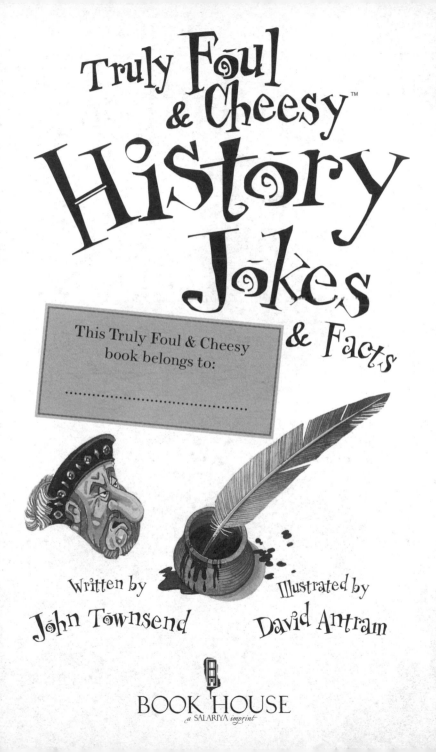

Truly Foul & Cheesy History Jokes & Facts

This Truly Foul & Cheesy
book belongs to:

....

Written by
John Townsend

Illustrated by
David Antram

BOOK HOUSE
a SALARIYA imprint

Introduction

Warning – reading this book might not make you LOL (laugh out loud) but it could make you GOL (groan out loud), feel sick out loud or SEL (scream even louder). If you're reading this in a library by a SILENCE sign... get ready to be thrown out for LOL-GOL-SEL!

The author really hasn't made anything up in this book (apart from some daft limericks and jokes).

He checked out the foul facts as best he could and even double-checked the fouler bits to make absolutely sure – so please don't get too upset if you find out something different or meet a world famous mad scientist/historian/total genius who happens to know better.

'If I had my way, I'd RATIfy the lot!'

5

History Secrets

Time is a funny old thing and there was always plenty of it about. In fact, time is nature's way of stopping everything happening at once! Looking at history helps us make sense of the past and put all that time in order. Without history, this wouldn't be now. Where would we be then? And they say we need to understand history so we don't make the same mistakes again. But somehow we often do. History seems to be a matter of one foul thing after another – so brace yourself for a yucky, disgusting and blood-curdlingly cheesy whizz through time. The past could be a scary place to hang out – in fact, it was often grim, gross, grubby, grisly, grotty, gruesome and grotesque – just like this book!

WARNING: necks get chopped a lot in this book – so you'd better keep your head down.

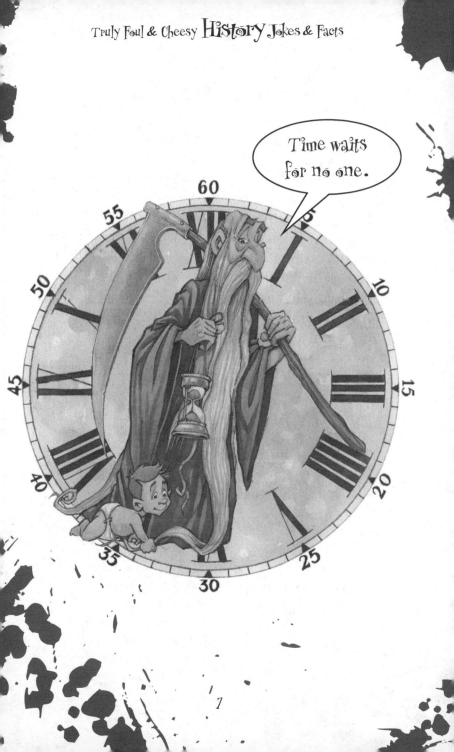

Back to Another Age...

The Stone Age was a scary time to live. 20,000 years ago, Earth wasn't just full of ice (after freezing long ice ages, brrrr) but also big predators like sabre-toothed cats, cave bears and lions. People had to hunt, too – even huge prey like woolly mammoths. The Stone Age ended between 6000 BC and 2500 BC, as around this time stone tools were replaced by tools made with copper. This was the Bronze Age, which led to The Iron Age from around 1000 BC to The Roman Empire. (After all, without the Iron Age, the Romans wouldn't have had such neatly pressed togas!)

Joke

Teacher: Which age followed the Stone Age and the Bronze Age? Here's a clue; fire, heat, solid and brown.

Pupil: That's easy. The Saus-Age.

A Stone Age Play

Stone Age Woman: Come quick – my mother's outside the cave where there's a dirty great sabre-tooth tiger on the prowl.

Stone Age Man: But I'm busy painting the walls of our bedroom.

Stone Age Woman: I told you I wanted magnolia – not a great big buffalo jumping a river.

Stone Age Man: You said you wanted a bison with running water.

Stone Age Woman: I said 'a basin'. I want an en-suite with ivory taps.

Stone Age Man: That's a mammoth job!

Stone Age Woman: Go and catch one, then.

Stone Age Man: Oh no – did you hear that terrifying roar?

Stone Age Woman: Get outside quick and see to my mother.

Stone Age Man: I've never heard her roar like that before.

Stone Age Woman: And see to that dirty great sabre-tooth tiger. Grab your club.

Stone Age Man: What do you want me to do?

Stone Age Woman: Just stop that savage causing a massive bloodbath.

Stone Age Man: I can't do that. You know what your mum's like when she's hungry.

Stone Age Woman: If you don't save the tiger, sabre-tooths could end up extinct.

Stone Age Man: What's extinct? What's a bloodbath?

Stone Age Woman: Hey – talking of bloodbaths, I've just had a better idea for the en suite...

Stone Age Man: Oh no – whatever's coming next?

Stone Age Woman: The Bronze Age, of course. A bronze bath with bronze taps would be just perfect.

Stone Age Man: Doh!

Grisly Fact

The remains of a young man buried with spears sticking out of his body 'like a hedgehog' was discovered in 2016 in an Iron Age burial site in Yorkshire. True. At first, archaeologists couldn't see the point – although they found several stuck in his skeleton! By the way, did you know an archaeologist is a person whose career lies in ruins?

Silly Riddle

Why did the mammoth have a woolly coat?
Because it would have looked ridiculous in an anorak.

Rat 1: What happened when the wheel was invented in about **3500 BC**?

Rat 2: It started a revolution.

Rat 1: A wheel was hard to make with stone tools.

Rat 2: That's because it took ages to get round to it.

The Stone Age was a rocky time - I preferred the Garb Age (That's a rubbish joke!)

Rat 1: Do you know what happened
       when the first caveman made
       a wheel?
Rat 2: Yep – another caveman drove
       by on a bike and stole it.
Rat 1: Doh!

I wish someone
would invent tyres and
a soft saddle.

Ancient Egypt (3000-30BC)

An Old Limerick
(first seen in ancient hieroglyphics):

(Decoded)
Hieroglyphics in pyramid tombs
Of ancient Egypt's catacombs
Have just been translated,
Their truths long awaited...
'NO SMOKING – WE DON'T LIKE THE FUMES'

Random Weird Facts About the Ancient Egyptians

Both men and women wore make-up in ancient Egypt and they liked clean teeth. At least, they invented toothpaste. It wasn't exactly minty fresh – but made of powdered ox hooves, ashes and burnt eggshells. How gritty and grotty!

Peasant children were set to work in the fields as soon as they could walk. They acted as scarecrows.

A 'cure' for blindness was to mash a pig's eye, mix it with red soil and pour it into the patient's ear.

For peasant children who wet the bed, their cure was a bag of mouse bones fastened round their neck. It also stopped the mouse bed-wetting, too!

In 1901 a British historian, Flinders Petrie, was exploring Pharaoh Djer's tomb. He found an arm wrapped in bandages that had been stuffed into a crack in the wall, perhaps by an early robber (an unarmed one, it seems!)

A Date With an Ape

Did you know that Egyptians made the first sweets? They came from dates picked from trees by trained baboons. The first ever monkey business?

Unwrapped, the bandages of an Ancient Egyptian mummy could stretch for 1.6 km.

How to prepare a mummy

The Egyptians believed their dead leaders (pharaohs) had to be mummified to preserve them for the afterlife. Here's the recipe:
Take one dead pharaoh and give it a good scrub
Remove all the organs, apart from the heart
Poke a long hook up the nose and mash the brain.
Pull out goo through nostrils
Stuff body with natron salt to dry out insides
After 40 days stuff with cloth and sawdust
Cover body in oils and wrap with long cloth strips
Place in stone coffin called a sarcophagus, seal tightly and leave to stand forever.
Job done!

No, you can't use the eyes for golf balls.

Scary Tutankhamun Tomb Tales (try saying that fast ten times!)

A tomb in The Valley of the Kings was discovered in 1922. Hidden inside was the mummy of the boy king Tutankhamun, with treasures and his golden death mask.

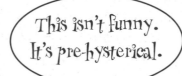

This isn't funny. It's pre-hysterical.

He became king when he was about ten in around **1333 BC** but died nine years later. Historians have never been sure how or why he died. Some said a hole in the mummy's skull showed he had been murdered. He also had broken bones. Other experts thought King Tut might have been killed by a hippopotamus, as Ancient Egyptians hunted hippos for sport.

Statues found in the tomb show him throwing a harpoon so maybe he was killed in a hunting accident. There again, he may have been killed by a chariot crashing into him. It's hard to be sure because he wasn't mummified properly as the body cooked and burned inside the coffin.

There were many mysteries and myths about Tutankhamen in both life and death. Lord Carnarvon, who funded the excavation of his tomb, died suddenly soon afterwards. As he died, the lights in Cairo failed and his dog back home howled. Superstitious people said it was a curse. Then, in 1944, a robber reached into another coffin to steal some gold. The lid fell and trapped him, then the roof fell in and killed him. They know when he died because they found that day's newspaper in his skeleton's tattered coat. Was this the mummy's revenge?

Slam!

Joke Time

Q. What do you get if you cross an Egyptian mummy and a car-horn mechanic?
A. Toot and Car Man.

Q. What does the 1333 BC inscribed on the mummy's tomb indicate?
A. The registration of the chariot that ran him over.

Q. What do you get in a 5-star pyramid?
A. A tomb with a view.

I love chariot racing. I always get such a kick out of it.

Q. Do you know why the ancient Egyptians never starved to death in the desert?
A. Because of all the 'sand which is' there!

Q. What do you call an Ancient Egyptian doctor?
A. Cairo-practor (A real chiropractor treats diseases by pressing a person's joints)

Newsflash: A mummy covered in chocolate and nuts has just been discovered in Egypt. Archaeologists believe it may be the first ever Pharaoh Rocher.

Are you winding me up?

Cleopatra: I want to bathe in a milk bath to keep me beautiful.

Attendant: But what if it turns sour and cheesy, your highness?

Cleopatra: There's nothing cheesy about the Queen of Egypt.

Attendant: Just wait till the end of this joke.

Cleopatra: Hurry up and pour pure ass's milk all over my body.

Attendant: Pasteurised?

Cleopatra: No, just up to my neck.

Attendant: Your skin is so beautiful, your majesty.

Cleopatra: No, not beautiful enough. You know
          what my psychiatrist said.

Attendant: Yes, you're the Queen of Denial.

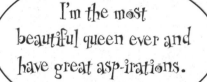

I'm the most beautiful queen ever and have great asp-irations.

Ancient Greece (2000-100 BC)

The Greek Empire was most powerful between 1000 BC and 146 BC. 776 BC was the year of the 1st Olympic Games. The ancient Greeks did many great things, had amazing ideas and some big brains. But one of them got well and truly clonked.

The Greek Philosopher, Aeschylus, came to a cracking end in 455 BC. He wrote many tragic plays but even he couldn't have imagined his own grim death. In fact, someone once told him he'd be killed by something falling on him, so he made sure he spent as much time outside under the clear blue sky. Big mistake. Along came an eagle carrying a tortoise for a take-away snack. But how do eagles crack open tasty tortoises? They drop them onto rocks. Mistaking Aeschylus's bald head for a rock, the eagle dropped the tortoise from a great height. Thwack! Neither tortoise nor Aeschylus survived. He was turtley dead.

Thud!

Slaves in Ancient Greece

There were times when slaves in Athens must have outnumbered free people.

There were several ways you might become a slave:
- kidnapped by enemy soldiers in wars
- kidnapped by pirates and sold into slavery
- born to slave parents

Slaves were sometimes treated badly. Some would be beaten if they tried to run away or if their owner was particularly grumpy.

Slave owner: Slave! Make my breakfast and bake the bread. Collect three sacks of salt and six of sand and use them for scrubbing all the floors. Then you must unload fleeces from the mule delivery. You will spin the wool and weave cloth to make my new clothes, a rug, cushions and a blanket. Be careful when working the loom. My husband got caught up in it and was badly hurt.

Slave: Is he all right now, madam?

Slave owner: Oh yes – he's completely re-covered! Next you will do the laundry, go shopping, cook our supper, fetch the water and oh, yes, make more olive oil, make cheese, collect the eggs, pick the fruit and milk the goats. I've left a list of other jobs for this afternoon.

Slave: (Unrolling a very long papyrus scroll) But all this is impossible, madam.

Slave owner: True – I was forgetting you can't read. It's all Greek to you!

Cheesy Fact

Did you know that Feta cheese is Greece's national cheese and is one of the most popular cheeses in the world? But what most people don't know is that feta dates back to ancient times. It's always been made from the milk of sheep and goats. In fact, the scary Cyclops (the one-eyed giant of Greek myth in The Odyssey) made sheep's milk into feta cheese even back then. How ancient and cheesy can you get?

Ancient Rome (750 BC - 476 AD)

Romans were a funny old bunch
Who'd stuff themselves fully at lunch,
Then go as spectators
To cheer gladiators
Who'd kill with a single swift punch.

Yes, not only did some rich Romans love to feast
on such delights as jellyfish, boiled ostrich, stuffed
sow's udder and flamingo boiled with dates, but
they'd also get a slave to bring round a sick bowl.
After all, they had to make room for pudding.

Don't bother to get up. You're about to become Roman history.

As for gladiators, who fought in arenas to entertain the crowds, they risked life and limb. If a gladiator was killed, there would be a rush of sick people to drink his blood and nibble his liver. They believed this would make them strong and fit. But that's not all. Women who were desperate for eternal youth collected the sweat and dead skin scrapings from gladiators and worked them into a facial cream. The cream was rubbed all over the woman's face in the hope it would make her look gorgeous and **DEAD ROMAN**tic (get it?).

This Gladiator Grease is called Drop Dead Gorgeous. He dropped dead and now I'm looking gorgeous.

Don't mention the toilets

The public toilets in Rome were often disgusting. Historians think they were never cleaned and full of parasites. Romans using the toilets would have to take in special combs for scraping out lice from their skin and hair.

Yikes - I've been bitten in the latrinium!

GROSS ALERT: Each public toilet, which was shared with dozens of other people all sitting together, would have a single sponge on a stick that you used to wipe your bottom. The sponge would never get cleaned – and you shared it with everybody else.

If that wasn't foul enough... creatures living in the sewage system would crawl up and bite people while they sat there. Rats could scuttle up between their legs. Not only that, methane gas could build up underneath, which sometimes got so bad that it would ignite and explode. What a way to go!

Doing the laundry in Ancient Rome could be fairly disgusting. It was the job of a 'fuller' to keep togas and tunics clean and white. So how did fullers do that? Simple – they soaked clothes in a mixture of hot human urine and water before trampling out the stains. The ammonia in urine helped with cleaning, and pots were left outside shops and public urinals to collect public pee donations.

My boss is the fuller. When I collect the piddle pots, he says 'make them fuller.'

Don't Try This At Home...

Some Romans were very keen on cleaning their teeth. They used toothpaste made from powdered mouse brains. In some areas, people used urine as a mouthwash, which they claimed kept their teeth shining white. Give us a wee smile!

When Romans weren't sloshing wee or gladiator blood in their mouths, some swigged a sweet energy drink containing goat dung. Charioteers were known to boil goat dung and vinegar into a drink or grind it into a powder. They gulped it down as a pick-me-up when they were exhausted. In fact, one of the most well-known lovers of goat dung refreshment was the crazy Emperor Nero. You wouldn't want to mess with him.

A quick warning about Nero (Emperor from 54 to 68 AD). Several Roman emperors were totally bonkers, horribly cruel or both. Nero was a nutcase. He didn't like his mother much so he tried to poison her – three times. Each time he failed so it was Plan B. He made the ceiling collapse on her. She survived. Plan C was to sink the ship she was on. She survived. In the end he sent his soldiers to stab her to death. What a nice man. When Nero tried to kill himself, he failed again. His servant had to finish him off instead.

Rat 1: I don't like to gossip – but I heard the emperor killed his mother.

Rat 2: I'm not surprised. She was a terrible woman and very wicked.

Rat 1: He had her cooked and served up for supper.

Rat 2: In that case, I'm gladiator!
(glad-he-ate-her)

Yuck – crocodile dung baths are a Roman beauty treatment. I'd rather stay ugly.

Roman medicine could be both foul and daft. How about these 'cures'?

- Slap a cobweb on a wound to stop the bleeding
- Rub tar and animal urine on the head to cure baldness
- Slap a nice piece of liver on the eyes if they get sore
- Kiss a mule's nostrils to stop hiccups (your hiccups, not the mule's)

More Foul Roman Facts

Mad Emperor Caligula had many people killed – often by sawing them in half.
Some criminals would be thrown to their deaths off the prison roof or from high cliffs.
Others would be buried alive or fed to the lions.

Riddle Time

Q: Who succeeded the first Emperor of Rome?
A: The second one

Q: What do you call a Roman Emperor with a cold?
A: Julius Sneezer.

Q: How did the ancient Romans cut their hair?
A: With a pair of Caesars.

Q: Where did Caesar keep his armies?
A: Up his sleevies.

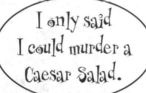

Saxons and Vikings (450–1066)

When the Romans left Britain around 450 AD, the Saxons left their homes in Germany, the Netherlands and Denmark to sail to Britain on wooden boats. Many of them were farmers looking for new land to farm. They were fierce people who fought many battles during their rule of Britain – different tribes fighting each other. But then the Anglo-Saxons had to deal with rampaging invaders from Norway – the dreaded Vikings.

From 793 AD, the Vikings invaded Anglo-Saxon Britain several times, plundering and raiding villages along the British coastline. The Anglo-Saxons tried to hold them back but groups of Vikings eventually settled in different parts of the country, especially York (or Jorvik, as they named it).

History Hip Hop

For peasant Anglo-Saxons,
Cow dung was all the rage
For building huts and growing crops
The smell defined the age.
Some people even sold it
To make a bit of cash
For where there's muck there's money, too
And that's not balderdash!
They also used their loo waste
For adding to the mix
To make a wattle and daub paste,
Just right with mud and sticks!
To be an Ang-loo-Saxon
(That's a joke but hey, it fits!)
They'd scoop out all the poo-holes,
That really was the pits.
But at least it helped with farming
And, if not to their liking,
Dung wasn't so alarming
As a foul rampaging Viking!

45

Vikings were quite keen on human waste, too. They would collect a fungus called touchwood from tree bark and boil it for several days in urine before pounding it into a pulp. The sodium nitrate in urine allowed the pulp to smoulder rather than burn, so Vikings could take fire with them as they travelled around.

Scrub up men. Get rid of that dreadful smell.

The Vikings were much cleaner than the Saxons as they had a bath every week. Saxons took a bath once a year. Apparently King Alfred once marched his Saxon army through a river because he couldn't stand the smell of his men.

Who's gonna tell him it's his horse that stinks?

Saxons sometimes skinned
Vikings alive and nailed
their skins to church doors.

Neither Saxons nor Vikings used toilet
paper. They used moss and leaves, and
sometimes their bare hands.

These
moss-wipes are full
of leeches!

Saxons sometimes sold their children as slaves, even under the age of 8.

Parents often picked a wife or husband for their child – who could marry at 12 years old.

It wasn't unusual for Saxon children to drink beer for breakfast.

Cheesy Joke

Did you know that the Anglo-Saxon leader Alfred the Great had something in common with Winnie the Pooh? They both had the same middle name!

Q: How did the Vikings send secret messages?
A: Norse code.

If you don't get the point of us Saxons, I'll soon show you...

Grisly Fact

King Edmund was a Saxon king of East Anglia until Viking invaders captured him in 870 AD. He was ordered to give up his Christian faith and share power with the pagan Vikings, but he refused. Instead of saying 'never mind, then', the Vikings tied Edmund to a tree and shot him with arrows, cut him open to pull out his lungs, then cut off his head. What a friendly bunch.

Keeping an eye out for the enemy

1066 saw the last Saxon king of England but King Harold didn't see it coming. He was killed by an arrow in his eye at the Battle of Hastings. Apparently his last words were, 'I spy with my little eye something beginning with "A"'. Led by William the Conqueror, the Normans invaded from France and it was the time many historians call the start of Medieval England.

Agghh!

The Middle Ages

Food in the Middle Ages was mostly
vegetables and porridge unless you were rich.
Guess what they sometimes ate?
(Brace yourself...)

———————

Stuffed porpoise stomach

•

*Deer antler soup – singed antlers
chopped in boiled wine*

•

*Mashed deer tongues – served on a
bed of fried bread*

•

Puffin with beaver tail

•

Sorry, no fries

———————

For The Record

For the first part of the Middle Ages, you only had to remember first names, as surnames did not exist. Then, when surnames were introduced you could pick your own. This was usually a nickname and could be anything. People often used their hair colour, a particular physical feature or a trade. It wasn't until several years later that surnames were carried on through a family via the father. Whatever happened to Mister Brownbigbottombaker?

A Pain In The Neck

In the Middle Ages people believed that a touch from royalty could heal a disease known as scrofula or the 'king's evil'. Scrofula caused swelling of the lymph nodes in the neck caused by tuberculosis. One treatment was this: 'When the king's evil develops, cut the swellings so that pus comes out. The scrofula should be scraped with a hook and drawn out.' Ouch.

Sorry to be a pain in the neck, but just grab my hand, your majesty.

Limerick Time

If you had the disease called 'king's evil',
Your puffed neck could cause an upheaval.
No local physician
Could cure your condition…
Just a touch from the king – how medieval!

The Black Death

The 1300s were a gross time for disease around the world. A deadly plague spread from China across the whole of Europe, beginning in 1328 and lasting about 25 years, though there were several smaller outbreaks over the next 60 years. About 200 million people were killed, reducing the world's population by a third. At its peak, 7,500 people were dying per day. One way this disease spread (often turning people's skin dark purple to black), was from bacteria in fleas. The fleas drank the blood of diseased rats, then hopped onto people, cats and dogs.

When the fleas bit, they passed the disease into the victim's bloodstream. Once you caught the disease, you only had a few days to live. You would get severe swelling of the lymph nodes, bleeding in the lungs and vomiting.

In fact, Genghis Khan (Mongolian leader) catapulted piles of infected corpses at his enemies just to show he meant business.

Yikes! Is it the plague doctor or a passing vulture?

They said I'd be stuck here for a long stretch. These jokes are nothing but torture.

The Tower of Torture

A dreaded prison and place of torture in the Middle Ages was the Tower of London. You can still see some of the scary instruments used to punish prisoners there today. One of these was the rack. The prisoner's ankles and wrists were tied to it then pulled, wrenching arms and legs from their sockets. Within minutes the victim would be screaming in agony and ready to confess to anything – even if they were innocent of a crime. They'd do anything not to spend a 'long stretch' in a dungeon. Another type of torture was the opposite to a rack – but just as scary. Instead of stretching the victim, the 'scavenger's daughter' crunched the prisoner like a nut cracker. For anyone with a crush on the gaoler, it was just the job!

Bloodcurdling medicine

For many illnesses throughout history, the cure (so they thought) was to 'be bled'. Getting rid of bad blood was bound to make you better, right? That's why you'd pop down to the barber, who would cut you to smithereens or slap a few leeches on you to drink your blood. It was called bloodletting.

In medieval Europe, bloodletting was the usual treatment for everything from plague and smallpox to epilepsy and gout. As well as cutting hair, barbers would happily drain your blood by nicking a vein in the arm or neck. They also pulled teeth, cut off warts, lumps and limbs – for a fee. The red and white striped barber's pole is still used today as a reminder of those bloodstained towels hanging outside the barber-surgeon's shop.

Joke Time

A knight and his men return to their castle after a hard day of fighting.

'How are we getting on?' asks the king.

'Sire,' replies the knight. 'I have been robbing and pillaging on your behalf all day. We have burned down all the towns of your enemies in the west.'

'What?' shrieks the king. 'I don't have any enemies in the west.'

'Oops,' says the knight. 'Well, you do now.'

Silly Riddle

Q: Why were the early days of history called the Dark Ages?

A: Because there were so many knights.

Some people don't like cheesy jokes about the Middle Ages. They just don't find puns about medieval castles re-moat-ly funny.

A Longer Joke

(as it's been stretched on the rack)

A Texan was on a history tour of London by taxi.
'I just love your little old country with all its quaint medieval history,' he said. As they drove past the Tower of London, the cabbie gave a brief history on how William the Conqueror began to build the White Tower in the 1080s and it was added to over the following centuries. The Texan replied,
'Really? A little ol' place like that? In Houston we'd have that thing up in two weeks.'

Next they passed the Houses of Parliament where the cabbie again gave a brief history; how the building sits proudly on the banks of the Thames, built between 1840 and 1870. But within its walls is the Great Hall, all that remains of the medieval Old Palace built between 1097 and 1099 – it was the largest hall in England at the time.

'Well, boy, we put up a far bigger one than that in Dallas and it only took a month,' the Texan scoffed.

As they passed Westminster Abbey the cabbie was silent.

'Well? What's that over there?' asked the Texan.

The annoyed cabbie scratched his head and replied,

'I have no idea, sir. It wasn't there yesterday!'

More Fast Foul Facts

Two royal children were kept in the Tower of London by their Uncle Richard. He didn't want 12 year-old Edward V and his younger brother ever to become king. When Richard III became the King of England in 1483, the two princes were never seen again. Fishy!

Richard III was king for only two years until his death in the Battle of Bosworth Field during the War of the Roses in 1485.

527 years later, archaeologists uncovered Richard's body in a Leicester car park.

Joke(ish)

What did Richard III tell his
town planners who wanted to
build a car park in Leicester?

'Over my dead body.'

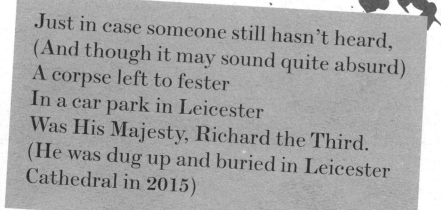

Just in case someone still hasn't heard,
(And though it may sound quite absurd)
A corpse left to fester
In a car park in Leicester
Was His Majesty, Richard the Third.
(He was dug up and buried in Leicester
Cathedral in 2015)

The Tudors

I'm looking for another wife. Anyone interested?

One of the most famous (and scary) families ever to rule England was the Tudors. They were in power from 1485 when Henry Tudor was crowned King Henry VII, until the time Queen Elizabeth I died in 1603.

King Henry the eighth was dead scary
And so was his daughter, Queen Mary.
They would chop off your head
And it has to be said,
No one was safe – so be wary.

Football

Tudors played a sort of football – but the goals could be miles apart and players often turned nasty. The ball was a blown-up pig's bladder and the rules were crazy.

It MUST be a foul... he just killed the ref.

This is how a Tudor writer described a game: 'Football is more a fight than a game... sometimes their necks get broken, sometimes their backs, sometimes their legs. Football encourages envy and hatred, fighting, murder and a great loss of blood.'

Creepy Cures

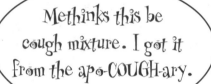

Methinks this be cough mixture. I got it from the apo-COUGH-ary.

72

Tudor medicine could be weird. They tried all kinds of daft potions such as:

- For gout – make a mixture of boiled worms, pig's marrow and a red-haired dog. Rub onto the foot and wait...
- For baldness – shave the head completely and smear the grease from a fox over the scalp. Crush garlic and rub in, then rinse with vinegar.
- For breathing problems – swallow frogs greased with butter. (Don't try this at home or you might croak!)

Foul and Filthy

Gross smells were all part of Tudor life. People rarely washed or changed their clothes and the rivers were open sewers. Tanneries boiled up animal hides to make leather and they pumped stinking gunk full of animal remains into rivers.

Toilets in Tudor homes were called 'privies' and were basically a bowl with a slab of wood and a hole carved in the top. In castles, a small cupboard-like area was called a garderobe. People would have to squat over a hole in the floor and their waste would plop straight into the moat below.

Peasants didn't have proper toilets – maybe a pot in the corner of the room. They would often relieve themselves where they could and then bury any waste matter. Washing hands after such a performance was not practised by anyone. Many would empty their chamber pots out of their windows with a cry of 'Gardez l'eau!' which is French for 'Look out for the water!' Our word loo may have come from this Tudor warning to 'dodge the wee'.

Neither rich nor poor had toilet paper.
Poor people would use leaves or moss to
wipe their bottoms. If you had a bit more
money then you would use lambs' wool
(but not with the lamb still attached!)

Chomp

Chomp

The toilets could hardly be cruder
For a desperate and foul-smelling Tudor
Who would squat in the street
And poo on your feet
Just what could be fouler or ruder?

Pain and Punishment

Public hangings were fairly common and not just for murderers. Even children who stole birds' eggs risked the death penalty. You could go out to watch prisoners being boiled alive in huge pots of water, or see the occasional beheading. Then on the way home, you could count the rotting heads of traitors stuck on poles as a warning to everyone.

I love this job - I'm really getting ahead in my career.

If thieves weren't hanged, they might have the letter T burned into their flesh with a red hot iron. Some criminals had their ears cut off or hands chopped off.

Tudors clamped rowdy troublemakers in a pillory in the middle of town. This was a wooden frame with holes for the head and hands, so offenders were stuck for all to see. The public could then hurl insults or rotten food at them. Splat!

Splat!

Head Cases

Even royals didn't escape the axe. Henry VIII was well known for having people close to him beheaded if they upset him. His second wife, Anne Boleyn, was only 29 when Henry decided to get rid of her. In 1536 Anne was taken to Tower Green at the Tower of London. She slowly climbed up all the steps to the scaffold to meet her executioner dressed in black. Anne spoke to the invited audience before kneeling with a blindfold. The executioner raised his sword and beheaded her with one blow. Legend has it that her lips were still moving when they lifted her head from the straw. Eeeek!

What shall I do today... change my vest, my palace or my wife?

The ending of the six marriages of King Henry VIII can be remembered by the rhyme:

'Divorced, Beheaded, Died –
– Divorced, Beheaded, Survived'

His other wife to be beheaded was Anne Boleyn's cousin, Katherine Howard (in 1542).

Look Away Now

As King Henry grew older, he grew bigger. Massive, in fact. He often had to be carried. He also grew more crazy and grumpy. The Tower of London became full of terrified subjects who had been imprisoned at his orders. Henry VIII sent more men and women to their deaths than any other monarch.

Next. Or should I say 'Necks-t?' Come on, chop chop...

One of the ghastly executions was of Margaret de la Pole, a 67-year-old countess, in 1541. She was ordered to place her head on the block, but she panicked and tried to escape. She was caught and forced back onto the block, where the executioner hacked at the poor woman's head and neck, only severing them after the eleventh blow. Ooer.

Quarrelsome Cousin Queens

For years there were no queens on the throne, and then three came along at once – all related and wanting the top job. That meant only one thing – more heads would roll.

Mary Tudor (1516-1558)

Queen Mary I of England was the daughter of King Henry VIII and his first wife, Catherine of Aragon. Mary reigned as Queen of England from 1553 until her death in 1558.

Catholics and Protestants were squabbling about all sorts and Mary didn't help much. She was a Catholic and put many Protestants to death, which is why she was called Bloody Mary. When she died, her half-sister, Elizabeth (a Protestant), became queen.

Actually, I was engaged to a Frenchman when I was 2½ years old.

I was also the first queen of England ever to be crowned. So there!

Mary Queen of Scots
(1542–1587)

This Mary (not to be confused with her cousin, Bloody Mary) was Queen of Scotland but she wanted to be Queen of England too, instead of her cousin Elizabeth. After all kinds of plots, Elizabeth had Mary arrested and eventually beheaded. Her execution needed two chops to her neck until 'the executioner cut off her head, saving one little gristle, which being cut asunder, he lifted up her head to the view of all the assembly and bade God Save the Queen.' (A bit late for that!) He was left holding her wig when her head fell and 'Her lips stirred up and down a quarter of an hour after her head was cut off'. Gross.

Elizabeth I (1533–1603) was the daughter of Anne Boleyn and Henry VIII. She was Queen of England from 1558 to 1603 and in all that time, hundreds of people were executed – many of them women accused of being witches. With Elizabeth's death from old age in 1603, the Tudor dynasty came to an end as she had no children to follow her.

I'm the foul-mouthed queen. I speak many languages and swear in all of them.

Cheesy Tudor Jokes

Q. When Henry VIII went to see his second wife after she gave birth to Elizabeth, how did he decide to enter the chamber?
A. Just amble in (Anne Boleyn, get it?)

Q. Why did Henry VIII have so many wives?
A. He liked to chop and change.

Q. Is there any proof that people played tennis in Tudor Times?
A. YES. Many people served in Henry VIII's Court.

When King Henry told a comedian to make him laugh or be executed, the man put on a funny hat and made a rude sign. It was the court gesture.

Q. Why is the ghost of Anne Boleyn always running after the ghost of Henry VIII?
A. She's trying to get ahead.

Q. What was the first thing Queen Elizabeth did on ascending to the throne?
A. Sat down.

Oops – spelling mistakes in an exam answer...

'Queen Elizabeth I never had peace of mind because Mary Queen of Scots was always hoovering in the background. She also knitted Sir Walter Raleigh on a ship.'

1600s

The Gunpowder Plot

In 1605 there was a plot to blow up James I, the first of the Stuart kings of England. He had upset many Catholics so a small gang, including Guy Fawkes, was set on revenge... (pause for scary music and evil laugh)... Although Guy Fawkes wasn't the main plotter, he had one of the most important jobs. A cellar below the Houses of Parliament was rented by the gang and they filled it with 36 barrels of gunpowder. That was enough explosive to destroy the whole building and many more in a one mile radius.

Guy Fawkes was in charge of guarding the gunpowder and of lighting the fuse. Unluckily for him, he was discovered in the act and captured. Within days, after being tortured, the gang was publically executed by being hung, drawn and quartered. Don't read the next bit if you are of a nervous disposition.

Once on the scaffold, the prisoners were hung until nearly dead. When they were cut down, their 'privy parts' were cut off before their innards were 'drawn' from them while they were still alive. These were thrown on a fire before they were beheaded. Their bodies were cut into quarters and these parts were displayed as a warning to others.

I'm just a normal GUY, honest. I hope they let me off (a well as my gunpowder).

Guy Fawkes Jokes

Did you hear about the two kids who made a guy and dragged it through the streets on Guy Fawkes Night? The police arrested them both; one for having a dead phone and the other for carrying fireworks. They charged one and let the other off.

Some people think Guy Fawkes was off his rocket. He was certainly bang out of order.

What was Guy Fawkes' favourite meal? Bangers and mash.

Theatre

As so few people could read and write in the 1600s, many went to the theatre to hear news, gossip and learn history. William Shakespeare was the famous actor, playwright and poet of the time, and he wrote a staggering 37 plays and 154 sonnets. He had to stop writing plays and turn to sonnets when plague shut down all theatres. Rats and fleas liked theatres, too!

To flea or not to flea?

Q: When did William Shakespeare die?
A: Just before they buried him.

(Actually it was 23rd April, 1616 – on his birthday, no less. Maybe he was so puffed out from trying to blow out the candle on his cake – so he snuffed it. He went from bard to worse!)

More Jokes

Did you hear about Shakespeare's set designer at the Globe Theatre? He got sacked for not doing anything but he seemed to take it well. He didn't make a scene.

Two people each claim to live in the building where Shakespeare wrote Romeo & Juliet.
There's a plaque on both their houses.
(Mercutio: I am hurt. A plague on both your houses!)

Shakespeare's leading comic actor fell through the floor during rehearsals. Apparently it was just a funny stage he was going through.

English Civil War

King James (who survived the gunpowder plot and ruled for another 20 years) died in 1625 and his son Charles I became king. He looked very fashionable with his long hair, neat beard and pearl earring, but he began upsetting more and more people by what he said and did. In a nutshell, he insisted he was the big boss with all the power, while Parliament said he had to do as they decided. Result = fisticuffs.

In 1642, people on the side of Parliament (called Roundheads, led by Oliver Cromwell) began fighting those on the side of King Charles I (called Cavaliers). This was civil war.

Some of the cannons used in the English Civil War were so large and heavy, they needed 16 horses to move them. Most of the time, they were used to scare the enemy as they weren't very accurate.

Boom!

By the time the war ended, it is thought 190,000 people died from fighting, and diseases caused by the fighting in England. In Ireland, over 600,000 people died from illness, famine and disease caused by the conflict.

King Charles I was executed for treason in 1649 and Oliver Cromwell was made Lord Protector, so he was now in charge and the war came to an end.

Look out – another beheading coming up...

King Charles was led to the scaffold which was covered in black cloth. He had asked to wear thick underwear so he wouldn't shiver, as the crowd would think that he was scared. It was said that when the axe came down and sliced through his neck, a sickening groan went up through the crowd. One observer described it as 'such a groan by the thousands present, as I never heard before and I desire I may never hear again.'

Spectators were allowed to go up to the scaffold and, after paying, dip handkerchiefs in his blood as it was thought the blood of a king when wiped onto a wound would cure that illness.

The next day, the king's head was sewn back onto his body, which was then put in a lead coffin. All mended!

Oliver Cromwell died in 1658 but three years later, his body was dug up to go on trial. Royalists found him guilty of treason and 'executed' him. Off came his head. Pointless!

1665 Plague

The summer of 1665 was very hot in London. Filth in the streets was worse than ever – a breeding ground for rats, fleas and disease. Plague returned on a scary scale.

By mid July over 1,000 deaths per week were reported in the city. It was rumoured that dogs and cats spread the disease, so the Lord Mayor ordered all the dogs and cats to be destroyed.

Over 100,000 people perished in and around London, although the plague spread beyond. Clothes sent to Eyam, a village in Derbyshire, contained the dreaded fleas. As the plague spread through the village, the villagers insisted no one must leave – or the plague would spread even further. Although they stopped the plague escaping, the villagers stayed and were wiped out; 259 died out of a total of 292.

The Great Fire of London

The plague in London was at last halted by a raging fire. In early September 1666, the Great Fire of London swept through the old city, destroying more than 13,000 wooden houses as well as 87 churches, including St Paul's Cathedral. It started shortly after midnight on 2nd September in Thomas Faryner's Pudding Lane bakery.

Samuel Pepys wrote about the raging blaze in his famous diary. His house in Seething Lane was in the line of the fire which was being driven by strong winds. Pepys was very worried, not just for himself and his wife's safety, but also for his gold, his wine – and his very special cheese.

Samuel: Dear diary.... (sighs – to himself) It's a new month, the first of September, 1666. My word, it's been a hot, dry summer. London has been baking. I've kept away from the centre of town where it is so dusty and smelly. I avoid it like the plague... Come to think of it, the plague avoided us, luckily. It struck down many hereabouts last year.

Elisabeth: Who are you talking to, Samuel?

Samuel: Ah, dear wife Elisabeth. I am recording a diary of our times.

Elisabeth: Can I have a look? Just a few peeps.

Samuel: Call me Samuel, not Pepys. You can
            use my first name after eleven years
            of marriage.

Elisabeth: And to think I married you when I was
            only fourteen.

Samuel: That's actually true, dear diary. And I
            was twenty two. Phew!

Elisabeth: Is something the matter, my dear?

Samuel: Can you smell burning? Has the maid
            overcooked something in the kitchen?

Elisabeth: I shall ask her. (Calling) Jane, can you
            come hither? It is almost midnight. She
            should be in bed rather than cooking a
            loaf. I hope the crust has not burnt again
            as it is hard for me to eat with my false
            teeth.

Samuel: (Whispering aside) That's true, dear
            diary. My wife is twenty six and has false
            teeth made of bone. Quite a fearsome
            sight at times, too.

Jane: (Knocks and enters the room) You called, madam?

Elisabeth: Are you baking, Jane?

Jane: I'm quite warm, yes madam.

Elisabeth: No, I mean are you cooking something in the oven?

Jane: Yes, madam – a fruit cake.

Samuel: Ah ha! I've just thought of a good riddle. What's fruity and burns?

Jane: I have no idea, sir.

Samuel: The **GRAPE** fire of London! (His laugh trails) No, I'm not sure that's funny, either. Maybe it will strike me as funnier tomorrow. And so to bed..

The next day, just hours later...

Samuel: It is very early on Sunday 2nd September. It smells as if Jane is already up and cooking something rather fiery.

Elisabeth: You're talking in your sleep again, Samuel. Blow out the candle and return to bed. It is only three o'clock in the morning. What's that smell?

Samuel: I don't think it is me, dearest. It must be the candle.

Jane: (Calling at the door) Sir, madam... the sky over the city is red.

Samuel: Then it should be a fine day later. You know what they say; 'red sky at night, shepherd's delight...'

Elisabeth: Or maybe the shepherd is on fire. Go and open the door in your night gown, Samuel.

Samuel: But I don't have a door in my night gown, dearest.

Elisabeth: Ask Jane what she can see exactly.

Samuel: (Opening door) What can you see exactly, Jane?

Jane: (Shocked) Ah! Your bare legs, sir. And no periwig.

Samuel: Spare your blushes, girl – where do you see something of real concern?

Jane: Through the window in the back room, sir.

Samuel: Then let me look. My word, there appears to be a blaze far off. I think it is the back side of Mark Lane.

Jane: I don't know **Mr Lane**, sir. And why would his backside be on fire?

Samuel: No, Mark Lane is a street on the other side of the city. It is far enough away and of no concern. Back to bed.

Within hours, the whole of London was ablaze.

In case you were wondering...
The cheesy end to Samuel Pepys's escape from the fire was a great relief. The large expensive Parmesan cheese he'd buried in his garden didn't get sizzled to a frazzle. When he returned to his house after the fire, his home was still standing and there in his garden, the ground was unharmed. Swaying in the breeze was a beautiful cheese plant. (OK, that last bit is a lie!)

Amazingly, not many people died in the Great Fire of London. Some reports said no more than sixteen. After the fire, the king (Charles II) ordered that London should be rebuilt, with buildings made of brick and stone instead of the wood that burned so fast. Christopher Wren was the architect in charge. It took ten years to rebuild.

And Finally...

How about a quick peep at the 'good old days' when most children didn't have to worry about school. How wonderful was that? Not much. The jobs children often had to do could be the foulest, filthiest and weirdest of all.

6 Of The Worst Jobs You Wouldn't Want To Do...

I'm always ill with the Flue (get it?)

Climbing Boy. If you were a chimneysweep's apprentice you'd be kept thin so you could climb up the narrow, sooty flues. Apart from starving, you'd suffer from lung and eye problems caused by all that soot, dust and smoke.

 Muck-raker. In medieval London there were no pavements, so everyone had to walk on the bare earth – which was covered with the poo of people and animals, as well as animal entrails and rotting food. Muck-rakers were hired to clean them as best they could. Not nice.

 Gong-scourer's Boy. Gong-scourers were hired to clean the private sewers of the wealthy. Their apprentices had to crawl down into the narrowest parts of these cesspits and scoop out the stinking sludge. These night-workers, who did the essential job of clearing human excrement from England's cesspits and privies, were restricted to living in certain areas. Unfortunately, they didn't get stinking rich from doing the job!

4 Barber's Apprentice. As well as cutting hair, barber-surgeons cut flesh for bloodletting and performed all kinds of gross operations. The apprentice got to mop up blood and dispose of yucky remains of operations – or maybe hold down the patients as they screamed. Collecting the leeches could involve letting the bloodsuckers latch onto their own legs – a way to lose dangerous amounts of blood.

5 Whipping boy. It might seem an easy job to be paid to play with a prince or princess. Your job would be to become a friend of a royal child or the child of wealthy parents.

But there was a catch. It was also your job to be punished instead of the royals, if they were naughty. It was the whipping-boy's duty to be punished in the place of a Tudor spoilt brat aristocrat!

Now you'll be whipped into shape!

Groom of the Stool. It was a great honour to do this job for the king or queen – to look after all the royal needs. Unfortunately, it involved assisting their majesties with bodily functions and washing. Yes, the groom of the stool was a royal bottom-wiper. Ah well, to get a good job, you usually have to start at the bottom...

And the rest, as they say, is HISTORY!

Rat 1: Don't you wish you'd been born 1,000 years ago?

Rat 2: Why's that – all the filth, disease and open sewers to enjoy?

Rat 1: Nah. If we lived 1000 years ago, think of all that history we wouldn't have to learn.

Rat 2: True. Did you do a headcount?

Rat 1: Of what?

Rat 2: The number of heads that got chopped in this book.

Rat 1: I lost count. Actually, some decapitation stories were so gross they had to be cut.

Rat 2: Doh!

QUIZ

1. What came after the Stone Age?

a) Bronze age

b) Platinum age

c) Old age

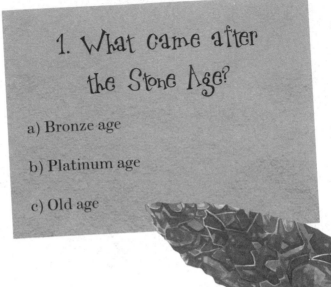

2. What did Romans use to wipe their bottoms?

a) The cat

b) A sponge on a stick

c) Triple-quilted toilet paper

3. Who was the last Saxon king of England in 1066?

a) King Harold

b) King Canute

c) King Kong

4. What was the Black Death?

a) A heavy metal band

b) A pirate ship

c) A deadly medieval plague

5. Who was the Groomer of the Stool?

a) The person who wiped a royal's bottom

b) Someone who cleaned the chairs

c) Someone who offered hair and beauty makeovers

6. Where were Richard III's remains found?

a) A Leicester car park

b) A flowerbed in Ipswich

c) A golf course in Surrey

7. Where were Egyptian pharaohs buried?

a) A landfill site

b) The Valley of the Kings

c) In the basement

8. Who were the two sides in the English Civil War?

a) Manchester United and Liverpool

b) The Eggheads and the Bandoliers

c) The Roundheads and the Cavaliers

9. How was Guy Fawkes executed?

a) Burnt on a bonfire

b) Publicly hung, drawn and quartered

c) Bored to death

10. How many wives had Henry VIII?

a) Four

b) Six

c) Three and a half

Answers:
1 = a
2 = b
3 = a
4 = c
5 = a
6 = a
7 = b
8 = c
9 = b
10 = b

GLOSSARY

Bacteria: microscopic lifeforms, which are usually single-celled and often cause disease.

Iron Age: a period of prehistory when humans first began to develop the ability to make tools out of iron. The period is generally held to end at the point when writing was first developed.

Leech: a type of bloodsucking, tube-shaped parasite that usually lives in water.

Papyrus: a material made from plant stems in ancient Egypt and used as sheets for writing or painting on.

Stone Age: a period of prehistoric time lasting for more than 3 million years, during which early humans made tools and other objects from stone.

Vikings: a seafaring race of people from Scandinavia who traded, pillaged and conquered throughout Europe in the 8th-11th centuries.

Woolly mammoth: a type of mammoth, which were large elephant-like animals, with a thick woolly coat that allowed it to live in very cold regions.

INDEX